CONNECTIONS

Pattie Palmer-Baker

Pattie Palmer-Baker

DREAM PANTHER

I am a panther.
I creep into your room when night oozes
black too thick to see through.
I slide in-between spaces
among your dreams and level my yellow gaze
at your most hush-hush self
pant my desire into your inner ear
and lick the whole of your inside,
grooming you for my indefinite stay.

THE PREY OF OUR EYE

I recognized the pilot straight away,
he must have broken through the silver screen
just before he cut his smile short, flew
right out of that theater and landed
next to the island to pluck us off the pier.

He flew us around and around
until the circles overflowed
with wrinkled navy blue ocean
freckled with fallen clouds.
We stretched our necks
turned our bodies inside out
hunting the prey of our eye,
a gray whale whose head would cleave
the sea and shoot a stream of white foam
as high as the aircraft.
We stared and stared into the ocean
rippling, glittering. No whales
but rocks like whales heads
jutted suddenly.

The pilot flew us around and around until the circles overflowed and away blue ocean freckled, fallen clouds. We turned our bodies inside out, having the prey of our eye, a gray whale whose head would dive deaf underneath. Flying journals of them streamed about, as we stared and stared. No whales but rocks like whales' heads jutted suddenly.

ODE TO A SNAKE

Sinewy strength once, the snake lies slack
its length checked by one loose coil.
Two yellow stripes race up the shining black
eyes glow ruby-red.
still something to look at, although dead.

When alive, a terrible beauty. No appendages
to interrupt his flowing length
undulating an S curve faster
than you can hold your eyes open.
If you touched him? Not slimy.
Enameled perfection,
pure musculature pulsing against your palm,
winding a sleeve up your arm.

Without a heart, though.
Something to remember
before you caress his scalloped skin
rub his satiny extent against your face.

My heart contract to see such terrible beauty stilled. Sinewy strength once. Now the snake lies slack, its length checked by one loose coil. Still something to look at, though dead, two yellow stripes rare up like slippery black eyes shine rubyred.

CANINE CHOIR

Listen to dogs howl.
They bring up the thing that aches,
fold their mouths in an O
and swirl a sound through the neighborhood
like black satin ribbon

unraveling.

My little dog sings
until the neighbor dogs join in.
Together, they accompany the siren's wail,
a gorgeous moan, their song,
in voices tenor alto and base,
an elegy streaming up the bitter sky

blacking out the stars lassoing the moon
pulling it out of orbit.

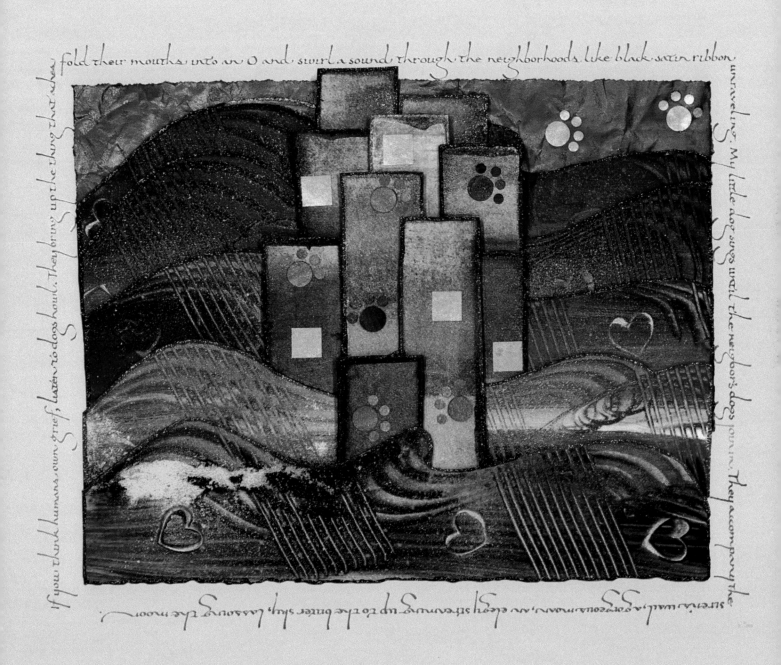

If you think humans own grief, listen to dogs howl. They bring up the thing that aches, fold their mouths into an O and swirl a sound through the neighborhoods like black satin ribbon unraveling. My little dog sings until the neighbor's dogs join in. They accompany the siren wail; a piteous moan, an elegy streaming up to the bitter sky, lassoing the moon.

JAPANESE POEM

Frothing gray-green anger,
the falls hurl branches, toss debris
careen down rage-carved stairs.

The alder gauges the height of falling grief
offers a spray of yellowing leaves,
a Japanese poem written above the spewing foam.

The waterfall tumbles into serenity, spreads
into the spaces between the fingers
of green-wristed black-gloved mountains.

A Japanese poem, unwritten, churns the glittering foam, and the waterfall rumbles into serenity; rages, but the alder tree gauges the height of falling grief; branches out over spray of yellowing leaves, anchored green, hurling branches; tossing delicate the falls careen down bedrock stairs carved by bedretad.

AUTUMN IS NOT FOR THE WEAK OF HEART

Autumn licks the maple's outer branches where green
heaves with desire for the sunlight smashing
stained-glass windows with red,
the long-wave extreme of the spectrum a heart pumps,

red wave after red wave but my heart beats
like a weak fist clenching, opening as wide
as a cracked door. Blood backs up,
a sticky red-black pool where tiny fists might float.
Doctors' fear, one will break loose and hurtle
to my brain, punch a black hole that sucks words, moons, worlds.

Only a little dangerous.
Not like *atrial fibrillation*, a serial-killer, pumps
wild erratic erotic. I would die for that rhythm.
Not this beat, weak, *organized into a saw-toothed pattern,*
inefficient, although symmetrical and pretty,
perfect for a woman clutching her heart for fear of.

Doctor's orders: *anticoagulant* to thin
syrupy black-cherry blood until watery red races
in my veins, pumping up blue centers
In the purple flowers my skin blooms.
Doctors warn my new blood, high on thinners
might overdose on red until I *bleed out*.
But why should I care? I am seasoned in autumn,
drunk on color.

THE TREES' LAST STAND, PART 1

Whores now, the trees strip green
to don orange sequins, red velvet and yellow satin.
Anything you want, the maple promises winter,
their pimp. He says, oh baby, just drop
a few more leaves around your trunk.
Sleeves bodices skirts fly off at a wind's notice.
Mmm, when you dress down to scanty
yellow netting, have you noticed
how that delicious part of you shines black?

Autumn: whores: now, these strip-*trees* a dozen times, are prostituted, *yet*, yellow-skin. Anything you want, the maples promise their pimp, *winter. Scarves, or dudes, skirts, fly at a wind's notice. Winter says, oh baby just drop a few more leaves, around your trunk. Mmm, dress-down is that scanty yellow netting.

THE TREES' LAST STAND, PART 2

The lace leaf maple whispers
I'll paint my face, smear my leaves with lipstick-red
anything that turns you on.
No use, winter tantrums, ripping snapping twisting
until the once layered lawn erupts chaos.
Leaves stained with red-orange blood
gush around the maple's slender trunk.
Winter grins, clacking and gnashing his teeth.

THE TREES' LAST STAND, PART 3

Birches, alders, maples cries to live on
burn so bright, they self-immolate.
The air wears sackcloth,
the fallen leaves bunch and buckle
spread brown and purple slime.
Bones now, the trees dream they are dead.
Winter exhales breath black with cold
studded with the lie
this is forever.

Birches, ash, maples' pleasure... leave on bitter soil...rends, the year is over...too. Whatever the trees discover they are dead: The air wears sackcloth, and the fallen leaves, hunch and spread down sticks to catch the first snowfall's detritus.

IN A BRONZE FIELD ALONE

You sit in utter stillness and warm
me with your amber gaze.
You are like a tree, an autumn tree
the sun backlights your leaves
Gold, carnelian and garnet.
your trunk is never bent, no bony arms
no sharp fingers reaching to the sky

I am here
for everyone's reason, right?
a failure to love.
I am a little girl
in a bronze field walking.
No one nothing
not even a tree is beside me.

My words float inside you
veins, heart, somewhere.

Hmmm. A rounded sound
then in a powder-soft voice
once you were a little girl
alone.
and yours is not a failure to love.
but a long ago failure to be loved.

You serve your words in tiny golden spoons.
I swallow
before I can hold them in my hand,
stroke them or lick them

I want to kiss your eyelids
stand you up and press my body
against your body.
Soft bruises will bloom
on our shoulders pelvis thighs.

CONNECTION CRAZY

I would give anything to see the solar-cyclone
rage in the northern sky, rip atoms from electrons
unleash freedom-frenzied photons to dance
the tarantella, sparking, firing, igniting the night
until the sky glows glass-green in the black-flattened air.

Maybe not anything. Not even for a friend
would I dig up my kidney for transplantation
although I think of myself as connection-crazy
longing for a joining as deep
as the stars in the northern sky.

Maybe for my sister.
We are already joint, veins, and cartilage-connected
so why not plant my kidney
in one who, when asked, warms
the part of me flattened black?

The heart is another matter
an organ I have torn out for maybe-husbands
who return it mangled, unusable
I have to grow another.

igniting the night until the sky glows glass-green in the black-flattened air. Maybe not anything. Not even for a friend. I would dry up a kidney, although I think of myself as a convective unit, longing for a jointing as deep as the stars in the northern sky. Maybe for my sister. We are already joined at the heart. And she lights my black-flattened part's humble glow, longing to see the solar cyclone raging in the northern sky ripping aloha's from electrons. Freedom-frazzled photons draw the tarantella

This book is dedicated to my poetry teacher, Dave Jarecki for his never-ending support, encouragement, and inspiration. Without him, this book would not have been possible.

And to my sister, Katie, for her well-thought out advice and outrageous praise.

And to my husband, Ron, for his patience and belief in me.

If you are interested in purchasing any of the pictured artwork, please contact the artist
info@pattiepalmerbaker.com

To read Pattie Palmer-Baker's bio or to view more of her artwork including artist-made cards, please visit www.pattiepalmerbaker.com

To order additional copies of this book, contact:
Xlibris Corporation
1-888-795-4274
www.Xlibris.com
Orders@Xlibris.com

Edwards Brothers, Inc.
Thorofare, NJ USA
August 2, 2011